I LOST MY BFF

TEACHER AND COUNSELOR ACTIVITY GUIDE

BOYS TOWN Press

Boys Town, Nebraska

by JENNIFER LICATE   Illustrated by SUZANNE BEAKY

I Lost My BFF Teacher and Counselor Activity Guide
Text and Illustrations Copyright © 2021 by Father Flanagan's Boys' Home
ISBN: 978-1-944882-68-6

Published by the Boys Town Press
13603 Flanagan Blvd.
Boys Town, NE 68010

For a Boys Town Press catalog, call **1-800-282-6657**
or visit our website: **BoysTownPress.org**

**All Discussion Questions, Worksheets,
and Activities are available for download.**

ACCESS:
https://www.boystownpress.org/book-downloads

ENTER:
Your first and last names
Email address
Code: 944882ilmbag686
Check "yes" to receive emails to ensure your email link is received.

Printed in the United States
10 9 8 7 6 5 4 3 2

Boys Town Press is the publishing division of Boys Town, a national
organization serving children and families.

TABLE OF CONTENTS

Chapter 1: My Friendship

Chapter 2: My Strategies

Chapter 3: Looking for Good in Others

Chapter 4: New Beginnings

TEACHER AND COUNSELOR ACTIVITY GUIDE

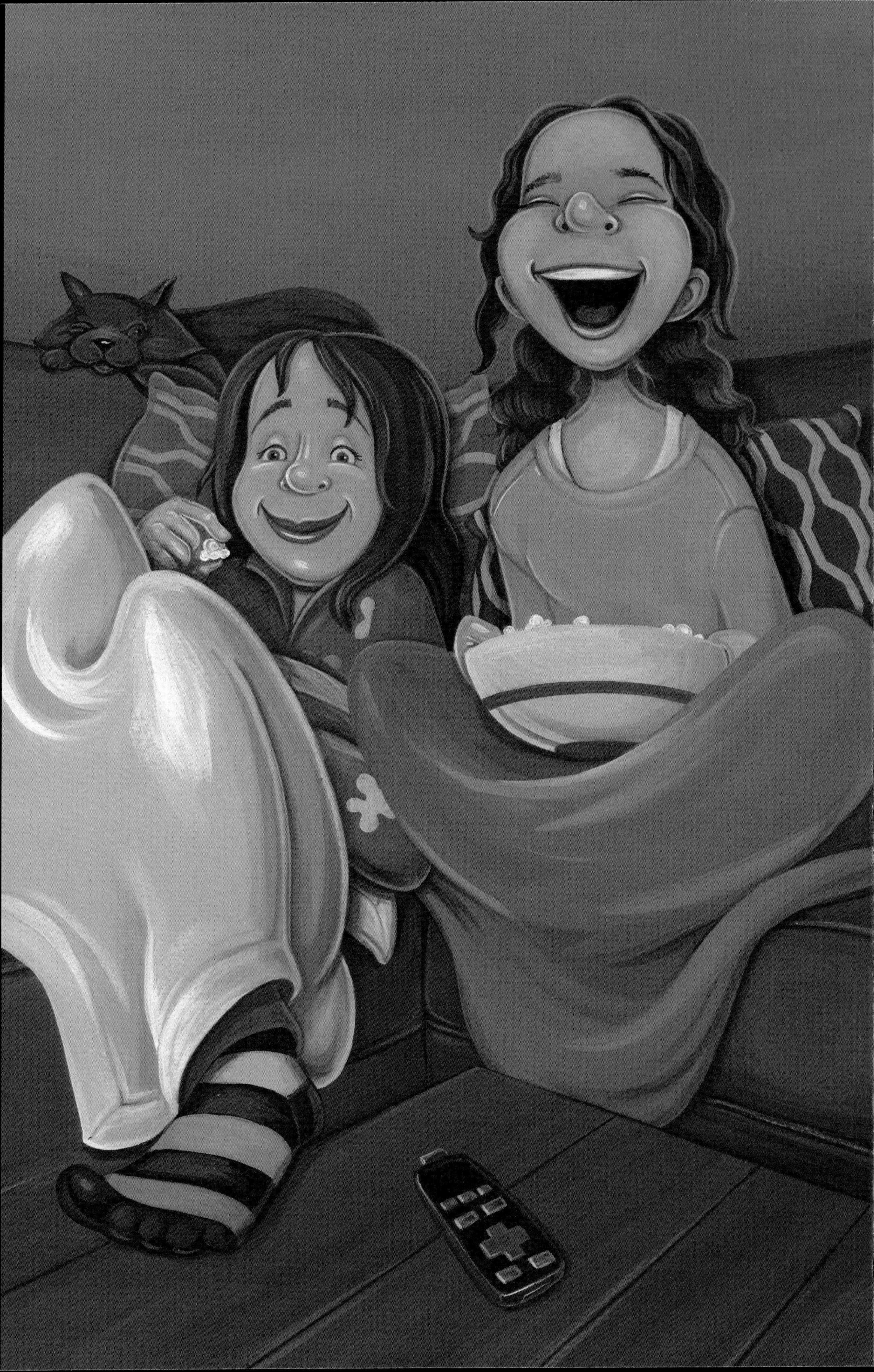

Chapter 1
MY FRIENDSHIP

MY NAME IS SOPHIA AND I HAVE A BEST FRIEND NAMED CAMILA. WE DO EVERYTHING TOGETHER AND HAVE SO MUCH FUN! WE WATCH MOVIES AND PLAY VIDEO GAMES TOGETHER. OUR FAVORITE THING TO DO IS IMAGINING WE'RE FAMOUS HOLLYWOOD SINGERS AND WHAT OUR LIFE WOULD BE LIKE! Even though we aren't in the same class this year, we get to see each other a lot at school. Every day we eat lunch together and hang out during recess.

I feel really lucky to have a best friend. I know I always have at least one friend so excited and happy to see me at school. I never feel nervous to walk over to a group of kids if she's there, because I know I'm always welcome. And, I trust her. I can tell her anything... funny stories, embarrassing stories, if I feel sad, dreams, goals I have for myself, really... anything.

And, I never worry she'll judge me or think less of me. I'm totally myself with Camila.

I haven't always had a best friend. When I was in kindergarten, there were only four girls in my class. The girls were always fighting about little things and it seemed like they were never getting along. I never knew who would be fighting by the end of the day. There was always some drama. That made it really hard to make friends.

Camila moved to my school in first grade, and she didn't like the fighting or the drama either. I was so excited to have a friend who felt the same way as I did. Camila and I just wanted to have fun, not argue about little things. We became friends right away and have been best friends ever since.

BUT LATELY, I'VE BEEN FEELING DIFFERENT. IT SEEMS LIKE SOMETHING HAS CHANGED WITH OUR FRIENDSHIP. SOMETIMES WHEN I WALK OVER TO CAMILA WHEN SHE'S WITH A GROUP OF OTHER KIDS, IT DOESN'T SEEM LIKE SHE'S SO EXCITED TO SEE ME. SHE'S STILL NICE, BUT SHE'S ACTING DIFFERENT. I'M WORRIED SHE'S MAD

AT ME OR THAT SHE'S NOT MY BEST FRIEND ANYMORE.

It was just a feeling I had until about a week ago. During recess, Camila told me she wanted to walk around on the track with Christabel instead of hanging out with me. Camila has never told me she'd rather hang out with someone else instead of me! It hurt my feelings! Why would she rather hang out with Christabel, instead of me, her best friend? She didn't even invite me to walk with them. I was too nervous and hurt to invite myself or ask Camila if I could join them. I didn't have any other friends to hang out with at recess because I always only hung out with Camila during recess. I spent the whole time walking around, looking for something to do. I didn't know what to do without her.

Being alone during recess was so sad and boring. But it got even worse. A few days ago, Camila invited Christabel to eat lunch with us. Why would Camila do that? We always ate lunch together, just us! Wasn't she having fun at lunch with me? Why wasn't our lunch good enough? Now, I'm not having fun at lunch, with Christabel sitting with us! Camila and Christabel are in the same class so all they do is talk about what happened in their class. They have all these inside jokes.

I'M LEFT OUT OF THE CONVERSATIONS SO I JUST SIT THERE QUIETLY. I was hoping they'd notice how quiet I was and try to include me in their conversation. But, they didn't seem to notice. One day, they spent the whole lunchtime talking about how funny their substitute teacher was. I tried to join their conversation by saying, "Tell me one of the funny stories." But they acted like they didn't even hear me. Even when I tried to join their conversation, it didn't work! It made me so sad it was even hard to eat my lunch.

My mind raced about the reasons why I wasn't being included. Were they purposefully ignoring me? Did they not hear me? I thought I said it loud enough. Why wouldn't they want me included in their conversation? Why does Camila even like Christabel? Does she like Christabel better than me? Why would she rather hang out with Christabel over me?

I don't understand why my best friend is acting different. Every time I try to hang out with them, I feel excluded. Do they even want me there with them or are they trying to show me they don't?

Why wouldn't Camila want to be best friends with me, like we were before? It's been making me sad and angry. Wait... is Camila really not my best friend anymore?

I am really confused and not sure what to think.

CHAPTER ONE

Follow Up Discussion Questions and Activities

Discussion Questions

1. Have you ever had trouble making friends?

_____

_____

_____

_____

_____

• Was there a certain situation where you had trouble making friends?

_____

_____

_____

2. Sophia was having trouble making friends when there was a lot of fighting and drama. Why do you think it would be hard to make friends in this situation?

_____

_____

_____

_____

_____

3. Have you ever felt like a friendship was changing, similar to how Sophia felt her friendship was changing with Camila?

_____

_____

_____

_____

_____

4. What changes did Sophia notice in her friendship with Camila?

    _____

    _____

    _____

    _____

5. What emotions do you think Sophia is feeling about the changes to her friendship with Camila?

    _____

    _____

    _____

    _____

6. Did you ever have a close friend who became friends with other kids, and you weren't happy about it?

    _____

    _____

    _____

    _____

Ask the students to share their opinions.

What are some strategies Sophia could use to respond to this change in her friendship with Camila?

Strategy A: What if Sophia calls Camila to talk about how she is feeling?

- Talk through how Sophia would express her feelings to Camila: "I have been feeling really hurt/sad/jealous/disappointed when you don't invite me to walk around the track with you at recess. It feels like things are different. How are you feeling?"

Strategy B: What if Sophia tries to be extra friendly with Christabel so she can become part of their group?

- Talk through the actions Sophia could take to be friendly with Christabel: e.g., Sophia could become friends with Christabel on social media. Sophia could ask questions about the stories Camila and Christabel are talking about when she is with them. Sophia could ask if she can walk with them on the track.

- *Discuss possible outcomes:* e.g., Sophia may feel happy to make a new friend and have her best friendship with Camila expand. Sophia may always feel left out. Sophia is ignoring her feelings and may feel this new friendship isn't her choice.

Strategy C: What if Sophia ignores the changes to their friendship and her feelings about the changes in hopes the situation improves?

- *Discuss possible outcomes:* e.g., Sophia will feel worse ignoring her feelings and not sharing them. The situation may improve on its own without using a strategy.

Strategy D: What if Sophia ignores Camila in hopes that Camila will ask her what is wrong? Sophia will be able to share her feelings. Will Camila then have an opportunity to share her feelings with Sophia?

- *Discuss possible outcomes:* e.g., Camila may misinterpret Sophia's actions and think Sophia doesn't want to be friends with her anymore. Camila may think Sophia is mad at her and may get mad at Sophia because she doesn't think Sophia has a reason to be upset with her.

- *Discuss possible outcomes:* e.g., Camila may misinterpret Sophia's actions and think Sophia doesn't want to be friends with her anymore.

Strategy E: What if Sophia invites Camila over to hang out or for a sleepover?

- *Discuss possible outcomes:* e.g., They will have a great time and their friendship will feel like it always has. Will their time together at the sleepover feel the same or different? Sophia may feel awkward about the changes in their friendship and act differently.

Friendship Exploration Activity

1. Choose Sophia's best strategy. Ask students:
   "What strategy do you think is the best option for Sophia?"

   - Strategy A, B, C, D, or E?

2. Break students into groups based on the strategy they chose (A, B, C, D, or E).

3. Have students brainstorm the benefits of their chosen strategy versus the other strategies.

4. Have students share with the class why they chose their strategy, including possible outcomes and how Sophia and Camila's feelings may change after Sophia chooses this strategy.

   - Depending on students' skill and age level, instructor could set up discussion as a respectful debate.

Notes:

_____

_____

_____

_____

I Lost My BFF

FRIENDSHIP EXPLORATION ACTIVITY WORKSHEET

STRATEGY	Benefits
A What if Sophia calls Camila to talk about how she is feeling?	
B What if Sophia tries to be extra friendly with Christabel so she can become part of their group?	
C What if Sophia ignores the changes to their friendship and her feelings about the changes?	
D What if Sophia invites Camila over to hang out or for a sleepover?	
E What if Sophia ignores Camila in hopes Camila asks her what is wrong?	

I Lost My BFF

WRITING ACTIVITY

There were two events when Christabel's presence created a noticeable shift in their friendship: 1) when she joined Sophia and Camila at lunch; and, 2) when Camila told Sophia she wanted to walk around on the track with Christabel at recess, instead of hanging out with Sophia.

- How did Sophia feel?
- How did Camila feel?

Tell students to choose one of these events.

- Take the perspective of either Sophia or Camila and write an end of the day journal entry, sharing the reasons for her choices and her feelings.
- Give students time to write these journal entries.
- Ask for volunteers to share their journal entry.

Discuss the responses as a group.

- Do students agree that this is probably how either Sophia or Camila felt?
- Do students agree on the possible reasons Sophia or Camila made these choices?

Chapter 2:
My Strategies

I HAVE BEEN REALLY WORRIED ABOUT LOSING CAMILA AS MY BEST FRIEND. I WOULD MISS HAVING A BEST FRIEND AND HANGING OUT WITH HER. SO, I DECIDED I NEEDED TO DO SOMETHING TO HELP OUR FRIENDSHIP. I'll just invite Camila over to my house. But I still have some doubts: If we hang out without Christabel, will things be back to normal? Maybe our friendship just feels different this year because we're not in the same class? Maybe we just need more time together for things to feel the same?

After school I saw Camila on the bus. "Hi Camila," I said in my most cheerful voice, even though I was a little nervous. "Hey Sophia," she smiled back at me and replied. "Camila, do you wanna come over to my house on Friday? Maybe you could even sleep over?" I asked. "That sounds like fun, Sophia, but I can't this Friday," she said. "Oh... ok," I replied. I wasn't sure if my face showed how disappointed I was, but Camila didn't seem to notice. She didn't even explain why she couldn't come over on Friday. Did she have plans with Christabel or did she just not want to hang out with me?

I was quiet the rest of the bus ride home. I couldn't think of anything to say after Camila said "No" to me. Camila didn't seem to notice I was upset. She just chatted with some of the other kids on the bus, while I was trying so hard to control myself so I didn't burst into tears. IT MUST BE TRUE, WE'RE NOT BEST FRIENDS ANYMORE. WHAT IF IT'S EVEN WORSE, WHAT IF SHE DOESN'T WANT TO BE FRIENDS WITH ME AT ALL? I wasn't sure how to fix things with our friendship, or if it was even possible? What will I do without her?

I was holding back tears the rest of the bus ride home. As soon as I walked in my house, I couldn't hold them back any longer and the tears just started streaming down my face. My mom hurried over and said, "Oh honey, what's wrong? What happened?" It took me a while to calm down, and my mom held me while I cried. I told her all about Camila and Christabel. My mom wiped away my tears and said, "I'm so sorry you're going through this. It's so hard feeling left out, especially by your best friend."

After my mom sat with me a bit, she told me a story about a friendship problem she had when she was younger. When my mom was about my age, her friend, Asha, started to exclude her from hanging out with her at school. It was very confusing for my mom because Asha would still hang out with her when they were home in the neighborhood but not at school. Mom was worried that the only reason her friend hung out with her at home was because there was no one else to hang out with. It hurt my mom's feelings to be excluded, even though it only happened sometimes. My mom didn't understand why someone who was such a good friend would act this way.

So, she decided to talk to Asha about how she was feeling, and it really helped. "How did it help?" I asked. "Well," Mom said, "she didn't know she had been hurting my feelings." Mom explained how Asha told her she was sorry and invited her to hang out with her at school too.

"Asha didn't even notice I was left out. I guess she thought I was hanging out with other friends. She didn't know how I was feeling until I talked to her about it," my mom added.

My mom stayed close friends with Asha and also became friends with Asha's new friends. My mom was glad she talked to Asha about how she was feeling because it helped her to not feel left out by her friend anymore. My mom and her friend found a solution to their problem.

Mom suggested, "YOU SHOULD TRY TALKING TO CAMILA ABOUT HOW YOU'RE FEELING AND SEE HOW SHE'S FEELING." My mom explained that it's a normal part of growing up to go through friendship changes. Mom said, "Some friendships won't last forever. As kids grow up, sometimes they change in different ways."

It made me feel a little better to know this was normal. "But I don't want to grow apart from Camila. I still wanna be her best friend," I explained. Mom replied, "Maybe you're not growing apart. Maybe the friendship is changing. Or, maybe it's something else you don't know about. Camila could be upset about something and this talk may give her a chance to share it with you. You don't know what's going on until you talk to Camila. Talking about your friendship is the first step to fixing it. You'll find out how Camila is feeling."

"Okay, that makes sense, hopefully it's just a misunderstanding," I responded. I was feeling hopeful for the first time in weeks. My mom gave me a big hug, and smoothed my hair as she said, "Take a few minutes to relax and then I want you to get started on your homework." I smiled and said, "Okay, I knew that was coming." My mom smiled back at me as she walked out of the room.

The next day, I took my mom's advice. I wanted to fix our friendship and have it feel back to normal. I waited until it was just the two of us and then talked to Camila about how I was feeling.

"CAMiLA," I SAiD, "I FEEL SAD AND ANGRY WHEN YOU LEAVE ME OUT OF THE CONVERSATIONS AT LUNCH AND WHEN YOU DON'T INVITE ME TO WALK AROUND THE TRACK WITH YOU AND CHRiSTABEL AT RECESS." Camila looked a little sad when I told her how I was feeling. She said softly, "I wish it didn't make you sad, but I really wanna have two best friends, you and Christabel. Sometimes I wanna hang out with Christabel at school. Maybe you could hang out with other kids when I'm with her."

I was disappointed by what she said and wasn't sure what to say. This wasn't what I was expecting. I was hoping it was a misunderstanding that we could talk about and easily fix. But, it wasn't! She doesn't want me always with her, like we were before.

After thinking about it for a minute, I whispered, "Okay, I understand." I told her I understood but I didn't. I didn't want to make more friends so why did she want to? And she doesn't want me with her when she's with her new friends. Wasn't I good enough?

CHAPTER TWO

Follow Up Discussion Questions and Activities

Discussion Questions

1. What strategy did Sophia first use to help her friendship problem with Camila?

_____

_____

_____

_____

2. What emotions do you think Sophia felt when Camila declined her invitation to come over to her house to hang out?

_____

_____

_____

_____

3. Sophia talked to her Mom when she was upset. Do you think it helped Sophia to talk about her problem?

_____

_____

_____

_____

4. What was the second strategy Sophia used to deal with her friendship problem when her first strategy didn't give her the desired result?

_____

_____

_____

_____

6. What emotions do you think Sophia felt after her conversation with Camila?

_____

_____

_____

_____

_____

• Why? _____

_____

_____

_____

7. What emotions do you think Camila felt when Sophia shared how she has been feeling about the changes in their friendship?

_____

_____

_____

_____

_____

- Why? _____

_____

_____

8. Have you ever felt sad and angry about a friendship?

_____

_____

_____

_____

- Ask students if there is a situation they have gone through with a friend that they would like to share (without using any other students' names).

_____

_____

_____

Notes:

_____

_____

_____

_____

_____

_____

_____

_____

_____

_____

_____

Role Play Activity

Act out how students would invite a friend over to hang out at their house.

- Complement/praise students for using positive social skills (e.g., Student says "Hi" to friend. Student asks friend if he or she would like to watch movies first before inviting him or her to come over and watch a movie.).

- Offer tips to improve social skills acted out during role play, if necessary.

Art Activity

Tell students: Draw a picture of a trusted adult you can talk to when you're going through a difficult situation or have a bad day.

- Draw that trusted adult in the setting you would feel comfortable sharing your feelings (e.g., Do you go fishing with your grandfather? Do you talk with your mother at bedtime?).

- Write or draw some topics it would be helpful to talk about with your trusted adult.

I Lost My BFF

DRAWING WORKSHEET

Draw a picture of a trusted adult you can talk to when you're going through a difficult situation or have a bad day. Are you in a special setting for this conversation?

Write or draw some topics it would be helpful to talk about with your trusted adult.

TEACHER AND COUNSELOR ACTIVITY GUIDE

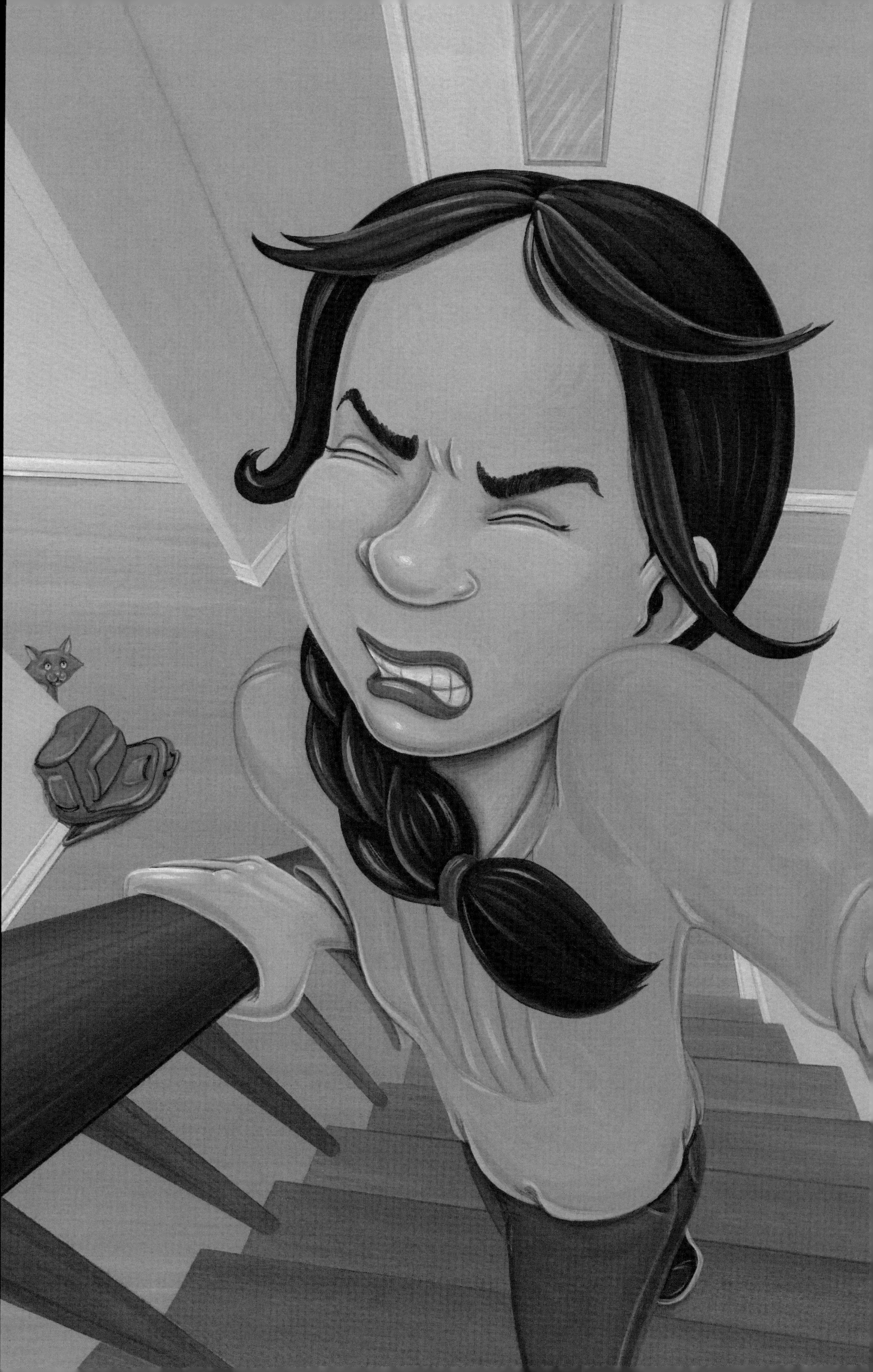

Chapter 3
Looking for Good in Others

After Camila told me she wanted two best friends, I came home from school upset... AGAIN. Everything will feel so different if I don't have Camila as my best friend. We were always together! Only us!

Now, I'll be left out whenever she's with Christabel. I was never left out before all this happened. I always had Camila. She was my best friend I could always count on. But, not anymore!

I walked into my house so frustrated. I threw my backpack on the floor, ran up to my room, and slammed the door closed. After a few minutes, my mom softly knocked on my bedroom door. She opened it slowly and tentatively asked, "How was your talk with Camila?" "It didn't help," I cried.

"SHE DIDN'T EVEN SAY SHE WAS SORRY. AND WHAT'S EVEN WORSE IS SHE SAID I SHOULD HANG OUT WITH OTHER FRIENDS WHEN SHE'S WITH CHRISTABEL. I don't have any other friends."

Mom hugged me and replied, "OH HONEY, I'M SURE THERE ARE OTHER KIDS YOU CAN HANG OUT WITH. YOU'RE SUCH A SWEET GIRL. ANYONE WOULD BE LUCKY TO BE YOUR FRIEND." My mom paused and then continued, "I'm sorry your talk didn't help the way you wanted but you did get to share your feelings with Camila. And, now you know how she's feeling. That's the first step to resolving a conflict."

My mom explained that Camila might not have known how I was feeling, and I didn't know how she was feeling. Mom said, "If you aren't honest with your friends about how you're feeling, situations don't have a chance of changing for the better. Talking to Camila was the right thing to do. But you also need to respect how Camila feels." My mom explained that even though it's hard, I have to let Camila have other friends and share her time with them.

It's not fair for me to expect Camila to only spend time with me when she wants to make new friends. "A friendship has to work for both friends," Mom said. "You two have always had such a great friendship, and Camila still wants to be friends, so you won't lose her friendship. But, the friendship needs to change so both friends are happy. A lot of friendships change as you get older."

My mom said I should look at this as a good opportunity to make some new friends of my own. Mom explained that things won't always go my way with friendships. Some friendships will end, even though you don't want them to end, and it'll be sad whenever that happens. My friendship with Camila isn't ending, but it has changed. If Camila wants the friendship to change, no amount of wishing from me will keep it the same.

"I know this situation will get better and you'll feel better, too. Try to think of some kids you have fun with at school, or some really friendly kids. I'm sure there are other nice kids you'd like to be friends with. Maybe some friends from dance class?" Mom paused and added, "I'll give you some time, and bring you a snack in a little bit." My mom gave me a hug. "Come see me if you need anything. I'll be back soon," she said as she walked out of my bedroom.

EVEN THOUGH I DIDN'T REALLY WANT TO MAKE NEW FRIENDS, I KNEW MY MOM WAS RIGHT. It would feel good to have other friends to hang out with when Camila is busy. But I am nervous to start new friendships. When my mom came back into my room with a snack, I told her in a frustrated tone, "I don't know how to find another best friend." Mom said, "You don't start a new friendship as best friends. That happens as you get to know a new friend. And, it's okay to have a lot of friends that you have fun hanging out with, and maybe one or two, or three best friends that you really trust.

Just look for kids you want to be friends with. Don't put pressure on yourself or on your new friend to try to figure out who you want to be best friends with. Over time, some friends will become best friends, and some just stay friends. All friends are important."

Mom and I decided I should call Jewel, a girl in my class that I'd always liked and had been friendly with. She used to take dance class with me. "Hi Jewel," I said when she answered the phone, "it's Sophia." "Hi Sophia," Jewel replied. After chatting a bit, I asked,

"Do you wanna come over on Saturday?" "Yeah, that sounds fun! Lemme check with my mom to make sure it's OK," Jewel said, as I heard her walking around calling out for her mom. I heard Jewel ask her mom if she could come over to my house, but I couldn't hear her mom's response. When Jewel came back to our conversation, she said, "My mom said it's cool and she'll bring me over on Saturday." "Awesome!" I said, "See you Saturday."

I WAS NERVOUS AND EXCITED FOR JEWEL TO COME OVER. I ONLY EVER REMEMBERED HAVING CAMILA OVER TO MY HOUSE. IT'S BEEN SO LONG SINCE I TRIED TO MAKE NEW FRIENDS. What if Jewel and I didn't have anything to talk about? What if Jewel was bored at my house? But, when I saw Jewel at school, I could tell she was excited to come over and that made me excited, too. We were hanging out more during school, too. One day during recess I was alone because Camila was hanging out with Christabel. Jewel came over to sit with me on the benches. I was so happy and relieved that Jewel saw me alone and wanted to hang out, or help me feel better. I didn't have to be alone during recess anymore. My mom was right, it felt better to have more friends.

When Jewel came over that Saturday, we had pizza and rode our bikes around my neighborhood. I had more fun with Jewel than I thought I would.

After Jewel left, Mom asked, "So, how was it?" I replied, "It was fun but not as much fun as when I hang out with Camila." Mom said, "It's normal for new friendships to take a while to feel as comfortable and to have as much fun together as old friendships." Mom suggested that I give the friendship time and that as I get to know Jewel better, we will have more and more fun together. Mom said, "NEW FRIENDS HAVE TO LEARN ABOUT EACH OTHER AND WHAT THEY LIKE TO DO TOGETHER. OVER TIME, THESE NEW FRIENDS CAN BECOME BEST FRIENDS, TOO."

CHAPTER THREE

Follow Up Discussion Questions and Activities

Discussion Questions

1. What was the advice Sophia's mother gave to Sophia when she was upset following her conversation with Camila?

_____

_____

_____

- Do you think it was good advice?

    _____

    _____

2. How did Sophia make a new friend?

_____

_____

_____

_____

- Brainstorm strategies to make new friends

    _____

    _____

3. Have you ever had to try hard to make new friends?   ☐ Yes   ☐ No

- What strategies did you use?

    _____

    _____

- Brainstorm situations where you will need to make friends because you may not know anyone.

    _____

    _____

4. What emotions do you think Sophia was feeling when she invited Jewel over to hang out?

    _____

    _____

    _____

    _____

5. What emotions do you think Jewel felt when she was invited over to hang out with Sophia?

    _____

    _____

    _____

    _____

6. Do you think it's important to have more than one friend?   ☐ Yes   ☐ No

    • Why or why not? _____

       _____

       _____

    • What are the benefits of having more than one friend or more than one group
       of friends?

       _____

       _____

Finding New Friends.

1. Ask students: Are there any friends you would like to be closer with? Think about friends you talk with or hang out with at recess and/or sit with at lunch but haven't invited over to your house.

    - Write the name of one person you would like to make an effort to become closer with. _____

    _____

    - Now write the steps you will take to become friendlier with this person and show them you care about a friendship with them. _____

    _____

    _____

    _____

    _____

    _____

Chapter 4
New Beginnings

EVEN THOUGH I WAS STILL GETTING USED TO THE CHANGES IN MY FRIENDSHIP WITH CAMILA, I WANTED TO MAKE NEW FRIENDS. I KNEW I NEEDED TO ACCEPT THAT FRIENDSHIPS CHANGE. I also wanted to become closer friends with Jewel. I like Jewel! I kept inviting her over to hang out and she had me over to her house, too. I was surprised how much fun we had when we hung out. My mom was right!

We had more fun together as we hung out more often and got to know each other better. Jewel loves to ride bikes and do things outside, just like I do. At recess, we like to play basketball or just sit on the benches and talk.

Even though I've become friends with Jewel, I'm still friends with Camila. Camila and I still hang out together but not as often. That feels okay to me. IT'S SURPRISING THAT WHAT I WAS

AFRAID OF FEELS OKAY NOW. I'M SO RELIEVED THAT I'M NOT SAD ABOUT THIS FRIENDSHIP CHANGE ANYMORE. I STILL CONSIDER CAMILA ONE OF MY BEST FRIENDS. I trust her and when we hang out together, we still have fun doing the same things we always have. We can talk and laugh for hours about our pretend lives of being famous Hollywood singers!

At lunch, sometimes I sit with Camila and sometimes I sit with Jewel. I have fun with both friends but for different reasons. When I sit with Camila, Christabel usually sits with us and I don't get mad about it anymore. When I sit with Jewel, her other friends Damian and Lorenzo join us. Through these lunches, I have become friends with Damian and Lorenzo too.

THEY'RE SO FUNNY. I'M SO HAPPY AND EXCITED THAT I'VE MADE SOME NEW FRIENDS AND HAVE TWO GROUPS OF FRIENDS I CAN HANG OUT WITH! When I decided to try to become friends with Jewel, I didn't expect it to lead to making even more friends.

I feel proud of myself that I don't get upset anymore when Camila wants to hang out with Christabel. My mom explained to me that I was being jealous of their friendship. Before all of this, I understood jealousy as wanting what someone else has. When you're jealous, you don't want anyone else to have what you want. You think you are the only one who deserves to have the nicest or best things. But I never knew you could be jealous of friendships.

I was jealous of Camila's friendship with Christabel. I wanted to be Camila's best and only friend. I was worried that if Camila made more friends, she wouldn't want to be friends with me anymore. Now I understand that I wasn't acting like a good friend to Camila. I was thinking about my feelings and not Camila's. GOOD FRIENDS DON'T GET MAD OR JEALOUS IF THEIR FRIENDS WANT TO SPEND TIME WITH OTHER FRIENDS. Good friends respect their friends' feelings and encourage them to grow and change. I want to be a good friend to all my friends.

I'M SO HAPPY I'VE MADE MORE FRIENDS! IT MAKES ME MORE COMFORTABLE IN SCHOOL. Now I try to be friendly with a lot of kids in school. You can never have too many friends! I have a great time hanging out with both Camila and Jewel. I used to worry about what I'd do during lunch and recess if Camila was absent. It was a pretty scary feeling. But now, even though I miss my friends if they aren't in school, I know I have other friends I can hang out with.

When I got home from school, I was thinking about how much I've learned about friendships and how I've become a better friend. My mom really helped me with this problem. I thanked my mom for her help. She hugged me and said, "You're welcome, Sophia. I love you and I'm always here for you any time you want to talk." "I LOVE YOU, TOO, MOM. IT MAKES ME SO HAPPY KNOWING I CAN TALK TO YOU ABOUT ANY PROBLEM."

CHAPTER FOUR

Follow Up Discussion Questions and Activities

DISCUSSION QUESTIONS

1. What were the benefits Sophia gained from making a new friend?

_____

_____

_____

_____

2. Do you think Sophia was more confident at the end of the story?

_____

_____

_____

_____

- Share with students that not only does being friendly with many people give you more confidence but so does overcoming obstacles like Sophia did with her friendship issue.

    _____

    _____

- Sophia was proud of herself at the end of the story. Why do you think she was proud?

    _____

    _____

3. How was Sophia acting jealous in her friendship with Camila?

_____

_____

_____

_____

4. What were some of the lessons Sophia learned through dealing with this friendship conflict?

_____

_____

_____

_____

_____

_____

_____

_____

_____

ACTIVITIES

Art Activity

1. Tell students: Draw a picture of yourself in the middle of the paper. Then draw a picture of all your friends around you. In the picture, either write or draw what activities you like to do with each friend next to his or her picture.

2. Next, draw a line connecting the friends that you can hang out with at the same time, meaning those friends that get along well with one another.

3. Follow-up questions to ask after the art activity:

   - How many friends are in your picture?

   - Have you included all of your friends?

   - Can you hang out with any of these friends at the same time (look at connected lines)?

   - Do you hang out with most of these friends separately?

   - Do you like to hang out with a group of friends or one friend at a time? Why?

   - Looking at your picture, would you like to make more friends or are you happy with the number of friends you have now?

Thank You Activity

Tell students: Write a letter to thank a trusted adult (e.g., parent, grandparent, relative, teacher, coach) for being there for you.

   - Share with students that we all need people around us to support us, and it is good to let those people know how much we care and appreciate them.

Notes:

_____

_____

_____

_____

I Lost My BFF

DRAWING WORKSHEET

Draw a picture of yourself in the middle of the paper.
Then draw a picture of all your friends around you. In the picture, either write or draw what activities you like to do with each friend next to his or her picture.

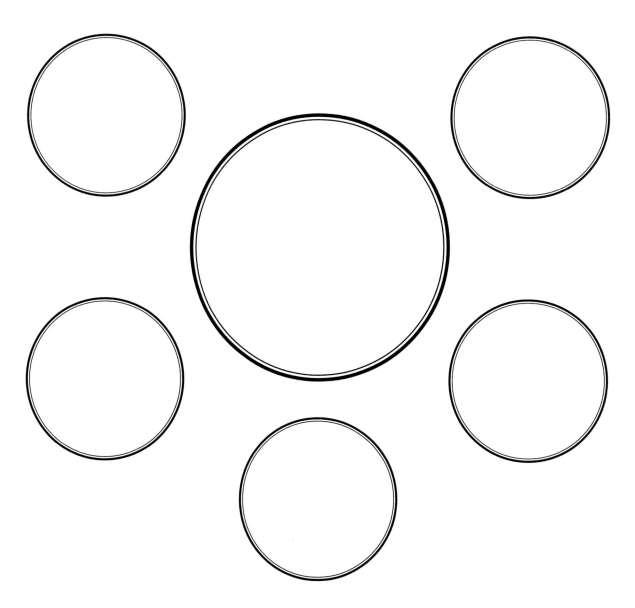

I Lost My BFF

THANK YOU LETTER

Write a letter to thank a trusted adult (e.g., parent, grandparent, relative, teacher, coach) for being there for you.

_____

_____

_____

_____

_____

_____

_____

_____

_____

_____

_____

_____

_____

_____

_____

_____

_____

_____

_____

_____

Boys Town Press Books
Kid-friendly books for teaching social skills

A book series and accompanying activity guides focused on changing friendships, finding your place, advocating for yourself, and being true to who you are.

978-1-944882-63-1

978-1-944882-64-8

978-1-944882-65-5

978-1-944882-66-2

978-1-944882-67-9

978-1-944882-68-6

978-0-938510-68-0

978-0-938510-69-7

Navigating Friendships
Jennifer Licate
GRADES 4-7

978-1-944882-94-5

978-1-944882-95-2

978-1-9444882-89-1

978-1-944882-90-7

A book series teaching important lessons about lying, cheating, and being a good friend.

978-1-934490-94-5

978-1-944882-03-7

978-1-944882-10-5

978-1-944882-21-1

978-1-944882-32-7

For information on Boys Town and its Education Model, Common Sense Parenting®, and training programs:
LiftwithBoysTown.org | parenting.org
training@BoysTown.org | 1-800-545-5771

For parenting and educational books and other resources:
BoysTownPress.org
btpress@BoysTown.org | 1-800-282-6657